200

Recipes and Rhymes

A CHILDREN'S COOKERY BOOK

ELAINE BASTABLE

PICTURES BY

Margaret Gordon

HEINEMANN : LONDON

William Heinemann Ltd
15 Queen Street, Mayfair, London W1X 8BE

London Melbourne Toronto
Johannesburg Auckland

First published 1975
© Elaine Bastable 1975
Illustrations © Margaret Gordon 1975

434 92844 5

10365

Printed in Great Britain by
Morrison and Gibb Ltd
London and Edinburgh

Thank you to Nicky (7)
William (8)
Julia (6)
Robert (9)
Arabella (7)
and
Harriet (10)
who so eagerly cooked and approved
all the recipes in this book.

Acknowledgements

The author and publishers would like to thank the following for their kind permission to reproduce rhymes on the pages indicated:

The Clarendon Press, Oxford, for 'The Quaker's Wife' (p. 43) from *The Oxford Nursery Rhyme Book* assembled by Iona and Peter Opie, 1955; A. Elliott-Cannon for 'Breakfast' (p. 46) from *Second Verse*, published by Johnston and Bacon; Evans Brothers (Books) Limited for 'If I were an Apple' (p. 67), from *The Book of a Thousand Poems*; Faber and Faber Ltd for 'A peanut on the railway track' (p. 16), 'Hippity hop to the baker's shop' (p. 85), 'Nose, nose, jolly red nose' (p. 82), 'One day a boy went walking' (p. 61), 'Wash the dishes' (p. 94), 'As I was walking down the lake' (p. 58), and 'An accident happened' (p. 25) from *The Faber Book of Nursery Verse*; Grosset and Dunlap Inc for 'Gingerbread Man' (p. 55) from *Favourite Poems to Read Aloud*; The Hamlyn Publishing Group Limited for 'Midday Feast' (p. 40) from *Sing a Song of Everything*; The Literary Trustees of Walter de la Mare, and the Society of Authors as their representative for 'Bunches of Grapes' (p. 76), 'The Cupboard' (p. 64), and 'Cherries, Ripe Cherries' (p. 19); Penguin Books Ltd for 'Pat-a-cake' (p. 28), 'Pussycat ate the dumplings' (p. 31), 'Rat a tat tat' (p. 49), 'Send Daddy home' (p. 52), and 'Simple Simon' (p. 73) from *The Puffin Book of Nursery Rhymes* compiled by Iona and Peter Opie; and for 'Careful Katie' (p. 37) from *The Puffin Book of Nursery Verse* compiled by Iona and Peter Opie; and for 'Mix a pancake' (p. 22) from *This Little Puffin*; Roberton Publications (for J. Curwen and Sons Ltd) for 'Honey spread on brown brown bread' (p. 79) by Edith M. Clark; Ian Serraillier for 'The Mouse in the Wainscot' (p. 34) from *The Tale of the Monster Horse*, Oxford University Press; William Jay Smith for 'The Toaster' (p. 13) reprinted from *Laughing Time*, Atlantic-Little, Brown, 1955, copyright © 1955 by William Jay Smith; The Society of Authors as the literary representative of the Estate of Rose Fyleman for 'Where did Momotara go' (p. 91).

CONTENTS

Introduction

Cooking is such a satisfying thing to do. . .

This book has been written with the enthusiastic co-operation of several young cooks, to make certain of success for all children. The recipes involve real cooking (for surely this is the most fun) but the methods have been simplified, so that they are well within the capabilities of a child.

Grown-up help will be needed at some stages by younger children, though as they become more confident occasional supervision will be enough.

There is magic waiting in the kitchen. I hope the readers of *Recipes and Rhymes* will enjoy discovering it.

Cooking with Grammes

You may like to cook using grammes and millilitres.

25 grammes is nearly the same as 1 ounce.
125 millilitres is nearly the same as $\frac{1}{4}$ pint.

Remember to measure either in OUNCES and PINTS or in GRAMMES and MILLILITRES, not a mixture of both.

OUNCES		GRAMMES
$\frac{1}{2}$ oz.	=	15 g.
1 oz.	=	25 g.
2 oz.	=	50 g.
3 oz.	=	75 g.
4 oz.	=	100 g.
5 oz.	=	125 g.
6 oz.	=	150 g.
8 oz.	=	200 g.
10 oz.	=	250 g.
12 oz.	=	300 g.

PINTS		MILLILITRES
$\frac{1}{4}$ pt.	=	125 ml.
$\frac{1}{2}$ pt.	=	250 ml.
$\frac{3}{4}$ pt.	=	375 ml.
1 pt.	=	500 ml.

A silver scaled dragon with jaws flaming red
Sits at my elbow and toasts my bread.
I hand him fat slices, and then, one by one,
He hands them back when he sees they are done.

HOT DRAGON TOASTS

3 oz. English cheddar cheese
Knob of soft margarine (the kind packed in tubs)
1 tablespoon of milk
Salt and pepper
2 large thick slices of bread
Watercress, if you have it

Makes 2

Have ready two warm plates.

Grate the cheese on the coarsest grater and put it in a basin. You may need a little help with this part.

Add the knob of margarine (large conker-sized), then the milk, and a good shake of salt and pepper. Mix them all together for a minute with a wooden spoon, to make a paste. Leave it ready.

Ask a grown-up to put the grill on high.

Put the slices of bread under the grill and watch them until they are toasted ON ONE SIDE.

Take them from the grill pan and spread the UNTOASTED side thickly with the cheesy mixture. Make sure you cover the bread and spread it right to the edges.

Put the slices back under the grill and toast the cheesy side for about 2 minutes until it is golden brown and bubbling.

Take them from the grill and carefully cut each slice in half. Put two halves on each plate with a sprig of watercress to make it look nice.

Read recipes all through with a grown-up before you begin.

A peanut on the railway track,
His heart was all a-flutter,
Along came a train—the nine-fifteen—
TOOT TOOT, peanut butter!

PEANUT FLAPJACK

2 oz. margarine
2 oz. demerara sugar
1 rounded tablespoon golden syrup
1 heaped tablespoon peanut butter, crunchy or smooth
4 oz. rolled oats
1 tablespoon salted peanuts

Makes 8

Ask a grown-up to put the oven on at 350°F OR Mark 4. Grease a round 7″ sandwich tin with margarine.

Weigh the margarine and sugar and put them in a saucepan. Measure the syrup and push it off the tablespoon with a wooden spoon into the pan. Put the pan on a low heat and stir with the wooden spoon until the margarine is melted.

Take the pan off the heat, measure the peanut butter and stir it in. Weigh the oats and tip them into the pan. Mix it well, then spoon the mixture into the tin.

Make your hand quite wet and lightly press the mixture flat. Ask a grown-up to chop the peanuts a little. Sprinkle them over the top and press them in.

Put the tin on the shelf above the centre. It will cook in about 25 minutes.

Use a thick cloth to take it from the oven, and while it is still hot, ask a grown-up to help you mark the flapjack into 8 equal wedges.

Leave it to get cold in the tin, then cut the wedges right through to lift them out.

Used saucepans filled with water are easier to clean.

'Cherries, ripe cherries!'
The old woman cried,
In her snowy white apron,
And basket beside;
And the little boys came,
Eyes shining, cheeks red,
To buy bags of cherries
To eat with their bread.

CHERRY CHOCOLATE PUDDING

1 (14 oz.) can cherry pie filling
Pudding mixture
4 oz. self-raising flour
2 oz. caster sugar
1 heaped tablespoon drinking chocolate
2 oz. margarine
1 large egg
2 tablespoons milk

For 4–6 people

Ask a grown-up to put the oven on at 375°F OR Mark 5. Grease the sides of a 6″ cake tin with margarine.

Let a grown-up open the can of pie filling. Spoon it into the tin and spread it evenly.

Now make the pudding. Weigh the flour and sugar and put them in a mixing bowl. Measure the drinking chocolate and mix it in.

Weigh the margarine and break it into small pieces in the bowl. Pinch the margarine into the flour mixture using the tips of your fingers. Keep turning it all over, making sure to reach the bottom of the bowl. Go on pinching and turning until the mixture looks crumbly all through. This is called 'rubbing in'.

Now rinse your hands.

Crack the egg into a cup and add the milk. Make a 'well' in the mixture and tip the egg and milk into it.

Use a wooden spoon to stir the egg and milk into the crumbly mixture, holding the spoon low down near the wide part. Mix it well. This will take about 4 minutes with rests. Now ask a grown-up to give it a brisk stir.

Take heaped teaspoons of the mixture and spoon them evenly over the cherries in the tin. You will find it easy if you scrape the mixture off one teaspoon with another. It doesn't matter if all the cherries are not covered and there is no need to spread it.

Put the pudding in the centre of the oven. It will bake firm in about 45 minutes.

Ask a grown-up to take the tin from the oven. Hold it with a thick cloth and turn the pudding out upside down on to a large plate.

Spoon on top any cherries left in the tin.

Serve the pudding hot. It is especially good with a chunk of ice cream.

Crack eggs into a cup first when adding them to mixtures.

Mix a pancake
Stir a pancake
Pop it in the pan,
Fry the pancake
Toss the pancake
Catch it if you can.

PANCAKES

Batter
1 egg
Pinch salt
$\frac{1}{4}$ pint milk
2 oz. flour, plain or self-raising
Cooking fat for frying
1 lemon, cut into 4
Dish of caster sugar

Makes 4

Have ready a small frying pan (7″–9″) and 4 flat plates.

Crack the egg into a basin and add the salt. Measure the milk carefully and pour it in with the egg. Weigh the flour and tip it into the basin.

Whisk everything together with a rotary whisk until the batter is smooth. This will take about 4 minutes with rests. Pour it into a jug. There is no need to let batter stand before using it.

Ask a grown-up to stay nearby while you make pancakes.

Put a knob of fat (marble-sized) into the frying pan. Melt the fat on a steady heat and let it get quite hot.

Pour a quarter of the batter into the hot fat—it should sizzle—then tip the pan from side to side until the batter coats the bottom. Cook the pancake for about 1 minute, keeping the heat fairly high.

Lift the edge of the pancake with a fish slice. If it is brown round the edges and set on top, it is ready to toss.

TOSSING. Hold the pan handle with both hands. Use a dry cloth if it's hot and keep the pan low down, level with your knees. Shake the pancake a little up the farthest edge of the pan—then quickly flip it over.

Tossing the pancakes is much easier than it sounds, but turn them with a fish slice if you prefer.

Now put the pancake back on the heat for half a minute to cook the other side.

Serve the pancakes on plates as you cook them. Each person adds a squeeze of lemon and sugar then rolls the pancake himself.

Lay a clean cloth on the floor in case a pancake misses the pan.

An accident happened to my brother Jim
When somebody threw a tomato at him.
Tomatoes are juicy and don't hurt the skin,
But this one was specially packed in a tin!

CRISPY CHEESE BEANS

1 small (7¾ oz.) can baked beans in tomato sauce
3 large thick slices of yesterday's bread
About 2 oz. English cheddar cheese
2 knobs of butter
Pepper
2 pinches mixed herbs

For 2 people

Ask a grown-up to put the oven on at 400°F or Mark 6.

Have ready a small (1–1½ pint) ovenproof dish and 2 plates.

Let a grown-up open the tin, then tip the beans into the dish.

Carefully cut the crusts off the bread, then cut each slice into tiny squares, like dice.

Grate the cheese on the coarsest grater. You may need some help with this part.

Put the knobs of butter (large conker-sized) into a small saucepan.

Put the pan on a steady heat until the butter melts and goes frothy, then take it off the cooker.

Tip the bread dice into the pan and stir gently with a wooden spoon until they soak up the butter. Add a good shake of pepper and the mixed herbs. Now mix in the grated cheese.

Spoon the mixture over the beans and spread it lightly to cover them. Put the dish in the oven near the top. It will cook crisp and brown in about 30 minutes.

Use a thick cloth to take the beans from the oven, and ask a grown-up to help you serve them on two plates.

A pinch is as much as you can hold between finger and thumb.

Pat-a-cake, pat-a-cake, baker's man,
Bake me a cake as fast as you can.
Pat it and prick it and mark it with 'T'
And put it in the oven for Tommy and me.

T COOKIES

3 oz. self-raising flour
2 oz. soft margarine (the kind packed in tubs)
1 oz. caster sugar

Makes about 15

Ask a grown-up to put the oven on at 350°F OR Mark 4. Grease a flat baking tray with cooking fat.

Carefully weigh the flour, margarine and sugar. (It is important to have exact amounts for this recipe.) Put them all together in a mixing bowl.

Squeeze the flour, margarine and sugar together with both hands until you have one ball of mixture. This will take about 4 minutes with rests.

Now rinse your hands.

Sprinkle a LITTLE flour on the table and tip the cookie mixture on to it.

With floury fingers, take small pieces of mixture and roll them between your hands into balls about the size of a big marble. Try to keep them all the same size. There should be about 15.

Put them on a baking tray with a space between each one. Flatten them a little with your hand, then prick each one once with a fork.

Put the tray in the oven on the shelf above the centre. They will bake pale golden brown in about 15 minutes.

Use a thick cloth to take the cookies from the oven. Leave them to cool on the tray for 2 minutes.

Now lift them carefully with a fish slice on to a wire rack to get cold.

Have you washed your hands?

Pussycat ate the dumplings,
Pussycat ate the dumplings.
Mother stood by and cried 'Oh fie!
Why did you eat the dumplings?'

PUSSYCAT BACON DUMPLINGS

1 (15 oz.) can oxtail or tomato soup
Dumplings
3 oz. self-raising flour
1 oz. shredded suet
Pepper
2 pinches mixed herbs
3 rashers rindless streaky bacon
5 tablespoons water

For 2–3 people

Have ready a medium-sized saucepan with a lid, and two or three soup plates.

Ask a grown-up to open the can of soup. Pour it into the saucepan. Fill the can two-thirds full with water, add it to the soup and stir them together. Leave it ready.

Now make the dumplings. Weigh the flour and suet and put them in a mixing bowl. Add three good shakes of pepper, *no salt*, and the mixed herbs. Cut the bacon into little pieces with scissors and put them in the bowl.

Stir it all with a fork. Make a 'well' in the middle and carefully measure in the water. Mix the dumplings with the fork into a very soft dough.

Tip it on to a well-floured table. With floury fingers divide the dough into six pieces. Roll each one lightly between your hands to make a round dumpling.

Put the pan of soup on a steady heat and stir it with a wooden spoon until it begins to bubble.

Now ask a grown-up to watch while you lower the dumplings on a tablespoon, one at a time, into the bubbling soup. Put the lid on the pan, lower the heat, and leave it to simmer gently for about 15 minutes.

The dumplings will grow quite large and come to the top of the pan when they are cooked. Ask a grown-up to help you ladle two or three dumplings into each plate and pour the soup round them.

Keep pan handles turned towards the back of the cooker.

Hush, Suzanne,
Don't lift your cup—
That breath you heard
Is a mouse getting up.

As the mist that steams
From your milk as you sup
So soft is the sound
Of a mouse getting up.

VERY SPECIAL HOT CHOCOLATE

2 heaped teaspoons drinking chocolate
2 heaped teaspoons sugar
$\frac{1}{2}$ pint milk
1 brickette vanilla ice cream
1 small bar flake chocolate

Makes 2 drinks

Have ready two mugs on saucers and two teaspoons.

Spoon the drinking chocolate and sugar into a jug.

Measure the milk and pour it into a small saucepan.

Put the pan of milk on a steady heat and watch it all the time until lots of little bubbles show on the top. Now it is ready.

Pour the milk carefully on to the chocolate and sugar.

Ask someone to hold the jug still, while you whisk it all together with a rotary whisk until a thick layer of froth appears on the top.

Pour the chocolate equally into the mugs.

Cut the ice cream in half and float one square on top of each drink.

Crumble the flake bar and sprinkle it on the ice cream.

Enjoy it right away.

Stand the jug on a low surface to whisk.

Careful Katie cooked a crisp and crinkly cabbage.
Did careful Katie cook a crisp and crinkly cabbage?
If careful Katie cooked a crisp and crinkly cabbage,
Where's the crisp and crinkly cabbage careful Katie cooked?

KATIE'S SAUSAGE HOTPOT

About $\frac{3}{4}$ lb. firm white cabbage
1 large carrot
1 small onion
Pepper
$\frac{1}{2}$ lb. skinless pork sausages
$\frac{3}{4}$ pint beef stock (made with 1 stock cube and $\frac{3}{4}$ pint water)
4 rashers rindless streaky bacon

For 3–4 people

Ask a grown-up to put the oven on at 375°F OR Mark 5. Have ready a $2\frac{1}{2}$–3 pint casserole dish with a lid.

Ask a grown-up to cut the cabbage into quarters and take out the stumpy part. Now lay the quarters cut side down, and with a knife carefully slice them into $\frac{1}{2}''$ wide strips. Rinse the cabbage strips in a colander and tip them into a big bowl.

Wash the carrot and grate it on the coarsest grater, then peel the papery skin off the onion and grate it like the carrot. You may need some help with this part. Put the carrot and onion in the bowl with the cabbage.

Add six good shakes of pepper, *no salt*, and mix it all together with a fork.

Now put half the vegetables in the dish and lay the sausages side by side on top. Cover them with the rest of the vegetables.

Ask a grown-up to make up the stock, then pour it into the dish. Lay the bacon rashers across the top.

Cover the dish with the lid and put the casserole carefully into the centre of the oven. It will cook in about 1 hour.

Ask a grown-up to lift it from the oven. With a big spoon serve the bacon, sausages, vegetables and gravy on to three or four deep plates.

Katie's Hotpot is very tasty with crusty new bread and butter.

Knives are sharp—be very careful.

Come on boys, look what we've found!
A dandelion all fat and round
And full of honey dew!
A midday feast, for bees who know
Good honey when they see it, so
Just tuck in
All of you!

HONEYBEE ORANGE

2 tablespoons honey, thick or clear
2 tablespoons sugar
½ pint boiling water
½ pint cold water
4 oranges
1 lemon

Makes 1¼ pints

Ask a grown-up to boil a kettle of water.

Measure the honey and sugar into a large basin.

Let a grown-up measure the boiling water. Pour it into the basin and stir with the tablespoon for a minute or two until the sugar and honey are melted.

Now measure and add the cold water.

Carefully cut the oranges and lemon in half across the middle, then squeeze out the juice on a lemon squeezer. You may need a little help to get every drop of juice out. Tip the juices into the basin—let the pips go in, you will be straining it.

When all the juices are added, pour the drink through a strainer into a jug. Put it into the refrigerator to get very cold.

Serve Honeybee Orange in glasses, with ice cubes and two straws.

Or very soothing sipped hot if you have a cold.

The Quaker's wife got up to bake,
Her children all about her.
She gave them every one a cake
And there the miller found her.

Sugar and spice and all things nice
And all things very good in it,
And then the miller sat down to play
A tune upon the spinet.

QUAKER CAKES

6 oz. self-raising flour
2 oz. caster sugar
3 oz. margarine
2 tablespoons chocolate drops (for cooking)
1 large egg
Icing
4 oz. icing sugar
1–2 tablespoons hot water

Makes 12

Ask a grown-up to put the oven on at 400°F or Mark 6. Grease a flat baking tray with cooking fat.

Weigh the flour, sugar and margarine and put them all in a mixing bowl.

Break the margarine into small pieces in the bowl. Now pinch them into the flour and sugar using your finger tips. Keep turning the mixture over, making sure to reach the bottom of the bowl. Go on pinching and turning until the mixture is crumbly all through. This is called 'rubbing in'.

Now rinse your hands.

Measure the chocolate drops and stir them in with a fork.

Crack the egg into a cup. Make a 'well' in the middle of the mixture and tip in the egg. Mix it with the fork, then your hand, into a stiff paste.

Dip your fingers in flour and take rough heaps of mixture about the size of a big conker. Put the heaps on the baking tray (try to keep them all the same size) leaving spaces between them. There should be 12.

Put the tray in the oven near the top. The cakes will bake rocky and brown in about 15 minutes.

Use a thick cloth to take them out and lift them with a fish slice on to a wire rack to cool.

Icing. Ask a grown-up to watch this part. Weigh the icing sugar and tip it into a small basin. Stir in 1 tablespoonful of hot water, then add the rest A LITTLE AT A TIME. Stop adding water when the icing is smooth and very thick, like golden syrup.

Drop a teaspoonful of icing on the top of each cake—don't spread it. Leave them for about 30 minutes to set.

First find everything you will need.

Bread and milk for breakfast
And woollen frocks to wear
And a crumb for robin redbreast
On the cold days of the year.

WINTER PUDDING

3 oz. left-over white bread, without crusts
$\frac{1}{4}$ pint milk
2 oz. butter
2 oz. sugar
3 oz. currants
3 oz. sultanas
2 teaspoons lemon juice
2 large pinches mixed spice
1 large egg
Caster sugar for the top

For 4–6 people

Ask a grown-up to put the oven on at 350°F or Mark 4. Grease a
$1\frac{1}{2}$–2 pint pie dish with butter.

Break the bread into little pieces and put them in a mixing bowl.

Measure the milk and pour it into a saucepan. Weigh the butter
and add it to the milk. Put the pan on a low heat until the butter
is melted into the milk. Pour the hot buttermilk over the bread and
stir it with a wooden spoon.

Weigh the sugar, currants and sultanas and tip them into the bread
and milk. Measure and add the lemon juice and the mixed spice.
Crack the egg into a cup, then tip it into the bowl.

Now take the wooden spoon and stir everything together until the pudding is well mixed. This will take about 2 minutes with rests.

Spoon the mixture into the dish and smooth the top with the back of the spoon.

Put the dish in the oven on the centre shelf. It will bake brown and crisp on the outside, but soft inside, in about 1 hour.

Use a thick cloth to take it from the oven. While it is still hot, sprinkle the top with caster sugar. Serve hot or cold.

Remember to turn the oven off.

Rat a tat tat, who is that?
Only Grandma's pussy cat
What do you want?
A pint of milk.
Where's your money?
In my pocket.
Where's your pocket?
I forgot it.
Oh you SILLY pussy cat!

NUTTY CARAMEL CUPS

1 (1 pint) packet caramel or chocolate blancmange powder
2 heaped tablespoons sugar
1 pint milk
For the tops
1 small (4 oz.) can cream
4 oz. nut brittle (from the sweetshop)
5 halves of glacé cherry

Makes 5

Have ready five small dishes.

Empty the blancmange powder into a basin, then measure and add the sugar.

Measure 2 tablespoons from the pint of milk into the blancmange powder and sugar. Mix it with a wooden spoon to a smooth runny paste.

Pour the rest of the milk into a saucepan and put it on a steady heat. Watch it all the time until lots of little bubbles show on the top. Now it is ready.

Carefully pour all the milk on to the blancmange mixture. Stir it gently round in the basin. Now ask a grown-up to tip it back in the pan.

Put the pan back on a steady heat and stir the blancmange all the time with the wooden spoon until it begins to bubble. Let it bubble gently, still stirring, for two minutes. Take it off the heat.

Leave it to cool for a minute, then pour the blancmange in equal amounts into the dishes. You may need some help with this part.

Let the blancmanges cool for 2–3 hours, or better still chill them in the refrigerator.

JUST BEFORE SERVING put the nut brittle in a polythene bag. Hold the ends tightly and tap it through the bag with a rolling pin to crush it into tiny pieces.

Let a grown-up open the can of cream. Tip it into a basin and stir it with a teaspoon.

Take the blancmanges from the refrigerator and spoon one big blob of cream into the centre of each dish.

Sprinkle crushed brittle over the top and lastly pop a half cherry in the middle. Serve straightaway.

Use a wooden spoon for stirring in a saucepan.

Send Daddy home
With a fiddle and a drum,
A pocket full of sookies,
An apple and a plum.

SOOKIES

5 oz. rich tea biscuits
4 oz. plain chocolate (for cooking)
1 tablespoon sultanas—if you have them
1 oz. butter
1 well-rounded tablespoon golden syrup

Makes 12

Have ready 12 paper cake cases on a flat tray.

Put the biscuits in a polythene bag. Close the ends of the bag and hold it tightly. Tap the biscuits through the bag with a rolling pin to crush them into tiny pieces. Leave them ready.

Break the chocolate into squares and measure the sultanas.

Now weigh the butter and put it into a saucepan. Measure the syrup and push it off the tablespoon with a wooden spoon into the pan.

Put the pan on a low heat and stir with the wooden spoon for a minute or two until the mixture bubbles and goes frothy.

TAKE THE PAN OFF THE HEAT and add the chocolate squares. Stir them gently in the hot syrup until they melt. Tip the crushed biscuits and sultanas into the pan, and mix until the biscuits are covered with chocolate.

Drop a tablespoonful of mixture into each paper case. Put the sookies in the refrigerator to set. They will be ready to eat in about 30 minutes.

Especially quick and easy to make.

A little old lady
Once took a flat pan,
And made for her husband
A Gingerbread Man.

The strange little man
Was made in this wise,
He had four currant buttons
And two more for eyes.

He was dressed in the brownest
Of little brown suits,
With little brown trousers
And tiny brown boots.

GINGERBREAD MEN

4 oz. PLAIN flour
2 oz. dark soft brown sugar
1 flat teaspoon ground ginger
2 oz. margarine
1 tablespoon milk
1 just rounded tablespoon black treacle

Makes 4–6

Ask a grown-up to put the oven on at 350°F or Mark 4. Grease a flat baking tray with cooking fat.

Weigh the flour and sugar and put them in a mixing bowl. Level off a flat teaspoon of ginger with your finger and shake it into the bowl. Mix it in with your hand.

Weigh the margarine and put it in a small saucepan. Measure and add the milk. Measure the treacle and push it off the table-spoon with a wooden spoon into the pan. Put the pan on a low heat and stir with the wooden spoon until the margarine is melted, then let it cool for 2 or 3 minutes.

Make a 'well' in the flour and tip in all the treacle liquid. Mix it into a soft ball using the wooden spoon.

Put the warm gingerbread on the table and begin right away to make the men. Roll small balls for heads and slightly larger ones for bodies. Put the heads and bodies straight on to the baking tray and press them flat with your hand.

Roll short lengths for arms and legs, then flatten these into place on the tray, just as you would do with plasticine. Leave a good space between the men so they can spread.

Press currants well in for eyes, nose and buttons.

Put the tray in the oven on the shelf above the centre. They will bake in 10–20 minutes, depending on how big you've made them.

Use a thick cloth to take the tray from the oven. Leave the men for 1 minute before lifting them carefully with a fish slice on to a wire rack to cool.

Try making this mixture into different shapes.

As I was walking down the lake,
I met a little rattlesnake.
I gave him so much jelly cake
It made his little belly ache!

SUNFLOWER JELLY CAKES

1 (1 pint) packet pineapple jelly
Boiling water
1 (11 oz.) can mandarin oranges
5 marshmallow sweets

Makes 5

Have ready five teacups.

Separate the jelly squares and put them in a measuring jug.

Ask a grown-up to pour boiling water over the jelly, up to the
½ PINT MARK on the jug. Stir it with a wooden spoon until the
jelly melts.

Let a grown-up open the can of oranges. Strain off the juice and
pour it into the jug with the jelly. Now add COLD water until
the liquid *just* reaches the 1 PINT MARK on the jug. Now you
have one pint of jelly.

MAKING THE SUNFLOWER. Press a marshmallow topside
down in the middle of each cup. Tuck 4–8 pieces of orange round
it for petals (the number depends on the size of the oranges). Keep
any left to use later.

Now spoon 2 tablespoons of jelly into each cup, then put them in
the refrigerator to set. They will be ready in 45 minutes.

Take the cups out and pour the rest of the jelly equally into the cups. Float any left-over orange pieces on top.

Put the cups carefully back in the refrigerator. Leave for 5–6 hours to set firmly.

TO TURN OUT. Have ready five small plates. Stand the cups in hot water for about half a minute to loosen the jelly. Hold each cup upside down over a plate—give it a good shake—and out it will come. Now you can see the flower patterns on top.

Wet the plates and the jellies will slide to the middle.

One day a boy went walking,
And walked into a store.
He bought a pound of sausages
And laid them on the floor.

The boy began to whistle—
He whistled up a tune,
And all the little sausages
Danced around the room.

HEDGEHOGS

½ lb. (4–5) large sausages
Knob of dripping
1 small packet potato sticks, matchstick kind
Box of mustard and cress

Makes 8–10

Snip the skin between the sausages with scissors to separate them, if necessary.

Put the knob of dripping (conker-sized) in a frying pan and stand it on a low heat until the fat is just melted.

Now lay the sausages in one by one. If you put them down gently the fat won't splash. Don't have the fat too hot or they will unzip their skins.

Let them fry slowly and turn them carefully with a fish slice now and again until they are brown all over. This will take about twenty minutes.

When they are cooked ask a grown-up to lift them on to a plate. Leave them to get cold.

Cut the sausages in half crossways, then push about nine potato sticks into each one to make them look like little fat hedgehogs.

Stand them on a plate and tuck small clumps of washed mustard and cress in between them.

Remember to wash your hands before cooking.

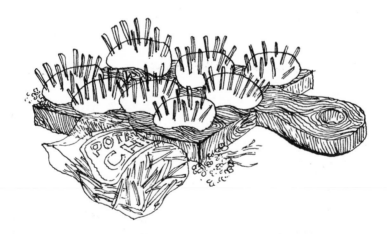

I know a little cupboard
With a teeny tiny key,
And there's a jar of Lollipops
For me, me, me.

It has a little shelf, my dear,
As dark as dark can be,
And there's a dish of Banbury cakes
For me, me, me.

FROSTY LOLLIPOP CAKE

1 large egg
2 oz. caster sugar
2 oz. self-raising flour
2 oz. soft margarine (the kind packed in tubs)
Frosty Topping
Juice of $\frac{1}{2}$ lemon
2 oz. caster sugar

Makes 8

Ask a grown-up to put the oven on at 375°F OR Mark 5. Grease a round 7″ sandwich tin with cooking fat.

Crack the egg carefully into a mixing bowl. Weigh the sugar, flour and margarine and put them in with the egg.

Stand the bowl on a low surface or sit with it on your lap, which-ever you find easier. Now mix everything together with a wooden spoon, holding the spoon low down near the wide part.

When the mixture is smooth and creamy (it will take about 5 minutes with rests) let a grown-up give it one brisk stir.

Spoon all the mixture into the tin, scraping it off the wooden spoon with a tablespoon. Now make your hand quite wet and pat the mixture flat.

Put the cake in the oven on the shelf above the centre. It will rise and bake golden brown in about 20 minutes.

WHILE THE CAKE IS BAKING, make the topping. Squeeze the lemon and pour the juice into a cup. Weigh the sugar, add it to the juice, and mix with a teaspoon.

Use a thick cloth to take the cake from the oven and turn it on to a wire rack. WHILE IT IS STILL HOT spoon the topping over and spread it with the back of the spoon.

Leave the cake for 30 minutes to get cold and the topping dry to touch, then cut it into 8 equal slices.

Let a grown-up watch while you weigh and measure.

If I were an apple
And grew upon a tree,
I think I'd fall down
On a nice boy like me.
I wouldn't stay there
Giving nobody joy,
I'd fall down at once
And say 'Eat me, my boy'.

APPLE POPOVERS

Batter
1 egg
Pinch salt
$\frac{1}{4}$ pint milk
2 oz. flour, plain or self-raising

Small Bramley cooking apple (about 5 oz.)
Caster sugar for sprinkling

Makes 12

Ask a grown-up to put the oven on at 450°F OR Mark 8. Grease a 12 hole tart tin thickly with butter.

Crack the egg into a basin and add the salt. Measure the milk carefully and pour it in with the egg. Weigh the flour and tip it into the basin.

Whisk everything together with a rotary whisk until the batter is smooth. This will take about 4 minutes with rests. Pour the batter into a jug. There is no need to let batter stand before using it.

Ask a grown-up to peel, core and quarter the apple, then you can cut each quarter into 3 chunky pieces. Now there are 12.

Put the tin near the top of the oven for $\frac{1}{2}$ minute until the butter is melted and hot. Use a thick cloth to take it out then pour the batter into the 12 holes, not quite filling them.

Put a piece of apple into each pool of batter. Ask a grown-up to put the tin back in the oven on the top shelf. The popovers will puff up and bake golden brown in about 15 minutes.

Take them out with the cloth, and slip them quickly on to a plate. Sprinkle them thickly with caster sugar and eat them warm, straightaway.

Lovely with golden syrup trickled over too.

I've made scones as soft and light as a dream
With red raspberry jam and thick yellow cream.
My best cups and saucers are ready you see,
For my friends are now here to take five o'clock tea.

JAM AND CREAM SPLITS

6 oz. self-raising flour
2 oz. margarine
3 pinches salt
5–6 tablespoons milk
Raspberry jam
$\frac{1}{4}$ pint double cream, lightly whipped

Makes 8

Ask a grown-up to put the oven on at 425–450°F OR Mark 7–8. Sprinkle a flat baking tray with flour.

Weigh the flour and margarine and put them together in a mixing bowl, then add the salt.

Break the margarine into small pieces in the bowl. Now pinch them into the flour using your finger tips. Keep turning the mixture over, making sure to reach the bottom of the bowl. Go on pinching and turning until the mixture looks crumbly all through. This is called 'rubbing in'.

Now rinse your hands.

Make a 'well' in the middle and carefully measure in 5 tablespoons of the milk. Mix to a soft dough with a fork. If the mixture is still crumbly, mix in another tablespoon of milk.

Tip the dough on to a floury table. Shape it into a ball, trying not to handle it too much. Roll the ball into a $\frac{1}{2}''$ thick circle with a rolling pin, keeping the round shape with your hands.

Brush the top with milk then cut the circle into 8 wedge-shaped pieces. Arrange them on the baking tray.

Put the tray in the oven near the top. The scones will rise and bake golden brown in about 10 minutes.

Use a thick cloth to take them out and put them on a wire rack to cool.

When the scones are cold ask a grown-up to help you split them in half with a knife. Spread jam on the bottom halves, then spoon a big blob of cream on top—don't spread it. Replace the scone tops and press them down gently.

Enjoy these on the day you make them.

Simple Simon met a pieman
Going to the fair.
Said Simple Simon to the pieman
'Let me taste your ware.'
Said the pieman then to Simple Simon
'Show me first your penny.'
Said Simple Simon to the pieman
'Sir, I have not any.'

SIMPLE SIMON PIES

8 oz. of your mother's pastry (or a small packet of bought short-crust)
1 small (7 oz.) can chopped ham and pork
Milk for brushing
Made mustard

Makes 12

Ask a grown-up to put the oven on at 425°F or **Mark 7**. Have ready an ungreased flat baking tray.

Let a grown-up open the can, then help you to cut the meat. Cut 4 thick slices lengthways, then cut each slice into 3 lengthways. (If it's a round can, first trim off 2 rounded edges.) Now you have 12 fingers of meat.

Sprinkle a little flour on the table and on a rolling pin. Make the pastry into a ball, then roll it out fairly thinly. Ask a grown-up to help if it rolls a little unevenly.

Take a 3″ plain round cutter, dip it in flour, then cut out as many circles from the pastry as you can, by cutting them very close together. Make the odd bits into a ball, roll it flat, and cut more circles. There should be 12 altogether.

Brush round the edges of the circles with milk. Lay a finger of meat across the middle of each one and spread with a dab of mustard.

74

Fold the 2 wide edges of pastry across the meat and overlap them firmly, like an envelope. The meat should peep out at both ends.

Brush the tops with milk and lay the pies on the tray. Put them in the oven near the top. They will bake golden brown in about 15 minutes.

Use a thick cloth to take them out and lift them with a fish slice on to a wire rack to cool—or enjoy them piping hot.

Wear a big apron and roll your sleeves up.

'Bunches of grapes,' says Timothy,
'Pomegranates pink,' says Elaine,
'A junket of cream and a cranberry tart
For me,' says Jane.

LITTLE FRUIT TARTS

8 oz. of your mother's pastry (or a small packet of bought short-crust)

1 small (8–10 oz.) can pineapple pieces, or any other favourite fruit

Jam Glaze

2 rounded tablespoons apricot jam

2 tablespoons pineapple juice

Makes 12

Ask a grown-up to put the oven on at 425°F or Mark 7. Have ready an ungreased 12 hole tart tin.

Sprinkle a little flour on the table and on a rolling pin. Make the pastry into a ball, then roll it out flat and fairly thin. Ask a grown-up to help if it rolls a little unevenly.

Take a 3″ fluted round cutter, dip it in flour, then cut out as many circles from the pastry as you can, by cutting them very close together. Make the odd bits into a ball, roll it flat and cut more circles. There should be 12 altogether.

Press the pastry circles into the holes in the tart tin and prick them three times with a fork.

Put the tin in the oven near the top. The tart cases will bake pale gold in about 10 minutes. Use a thick cloth to take them out and lift them on to a wire rack to cool.

Ask a grown-up to open the can of pineapple, and strain off the juice. Arrange the fruit in the 12 tart cases.

Now make the JAM GLAZE. Spoon the jam and 2 tablespoons of the pineapple juice into a small pan. Put it on a steady heat and stir with a wooden spoon until it begins to bubble. Let it bubble for 1 minute, then take it off the heat.

Ask a grown-up to pour it into a cup. When it has cooled a little, cover the pineapple in each tart with a teaspoonful of glaze.

Serve them as they are or with a jugful of cream.

Wipe up any spills as you go.

Honey spread on brown brown bread,
Nothing else I'll have instead.
Supper comes at nine—
I shall have for mine
Honey spread on brown brown bread.

BROWN BROWN BREAD

8 oz. plain white flour
8 oz. wholemeal flour
2 flat teaspoons salt
½ pint JUST WARM water
1 flat tablespoon of dried yeast
2 flat teaspoons sugar

Makes 12 rolls

Sprinkle a flat baking tray with white flour.

Weigh the plain and wholemeal flours and tip them into a mixing bowl. Measure and add the salt.

Now measure the water exactly, making sure it is only JUST WARM. Measure the yeast and sugar and stir them in. Go on stirring until all the yeast grains have disappeared.

Leave it to stand for 10 minutes until the top goes frothy.

Make a well in the middle of the flour and pour all the liquid in. Use your hands to mix it into a ball of dough and tip it on to a floury table.

Keep a *little* flour on the table and on your hands, then push and squeeze the dough until it gets smooth and bouncy. This is called kneading.

Now ask a grown-up to cut the dough into 12 equal pieces.

Roll each piece of dough round in your hands until it is quite smooth, then put them all close together on the baking tray. Leave just enough space to get your finger down between each one.

Lay a piece of greased polythene over the rolls and leave the tray in a warm place for about 45 minutes. During this time the yeast will make the dough grow to nearly twice its size. The rolls should now be touching.

While the rolls are growing, ask a grown-up to put the oven on at 450°F OR Mark 8.

Take off the polythene, then put the tray in the oven near the top. The rolls will bake crusty on top, with soft sides, in about 15 minutes.

Slide them on to a wire rack to cool, then break them apart.

Delicious newly baked, spread thickly with butter.

Nose, nose,
Jolly red nose,
And what gave thee
That jolly red nose?
Nutmeg and ginger
Cinnamon and cloves
That's what gave me
This jolly red nose.

WALNUT BURRS

4 oz. PLAIN flour
2 oz. caster sugar
2 oz. butter
3 pinches mixed spice
1 heaped tablespoon chopped walnuts
1 egg yolk
1 egg white, for brushing
Caster sugar

Makes about 15

Ask a grown-up to put the oven on at 375°F OR Mark 5. Grease a flat baking tray with cooking fat.

Weigh the flour, sugar and butter. Put them in a mixing bowl, then add the mixed spice.

Break the butter into small pieces in the bowl. Now pinch the butter into the flour and sugar using your finger tips. Keep turning the mixture over, making sure to reach the bottom of the bowl. Go on pinching and turning until the mixture looks crumbly all through. This is called 'rubbing in'.

Now rinse your hands.

Add the walnuts, then ask a grown-up to watch while you separate the egg. (See over the page.)

83

Tip the egg yolk into the bowl, cover it with the crumbly mixture, then squeeze it all together with your hands until you have one ball of mixture. Add a teaspoonful or two of milk if you need to.

Sprinkle the table with flour and roll the mixture on it with your hands to make a short fat sausage shape about 6″ long.

Now cut the roll into slices about $\frac{1}{4}$″ thick. Lay them side by side on the table. There should be 12–15.

Whisk the egg white with a fork for a few seconds. Brush each biscuit with it, then shake caster sugar on top, using a teaspoon. Arrange the biscuits on the tray with spaces between them.

Put the tray in the oven near the top. They will bake brown and crisp in about 12 minutes.

Use a thick cloth to take them out, and lift them with a fish slice on to a wire rack to cool.

To separate eggs. **Crack the egg gently on to a saucer. Hold the yolk back with a tablespoon and tip the white into a cup.**

Hippity hop to the baker's shop
To buy a stick of candy,
One for me and one for you
And one for sister Mandy.

LEMON COCONUT CANDIES

4 oz. icing sugar
3 oz. dessicated coconut
1 tablespoon evaporated milk
1 tablespoon lemon juice
Food colouring (yellow if you have it)

Makes about 36

Have ready a piece of foil on a flat tray.

Carefully weigh the sugar and coconut. Put them in a mixing bowl then add the milk and lemon juice.

Mix everything together with a wooden spoon, holding it low down near the wide part. This will take about 4 minutes with rests, and make a fairly soft ball of candy.

Now you can colour it. Dip a skewer into the colouring and shake 4–6 drops into the candy. Don't add too much, a pale colour looks best.

Press the colouring through the mixture with the wooden spoon until it is all mixed in. You may need a little help with this part.

Arrange teaspoons of candy in tiny rocky heaps on the foil. There should be about 36.

Now put the candies in the refrigerator to harden. In about half an hour they will be ready to eat.

Try not to lick your fingers!

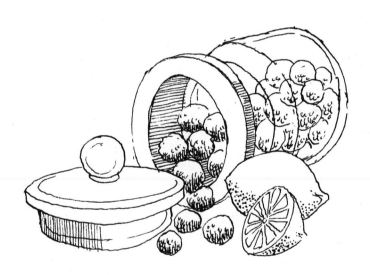

Bring on the porridge and the cream!
Those eggs look like a scrambled dream,
And my fried bread's the best in town,
So tasty crispy golden brown.
Some boys like dinner, some like tea
But breakfast makes a man of me.

MY FRIED BREAD

1 large slice of white bread, $\frac{1}{2}''$ thick
1 egg
1 tablespoon milk
Salt and pepper
Large knob of butter, for frying

For 1 person

Have ready a frying pan and a dinner plate.

Ask a grown-up to cut the crusts from the bread and show you how
to cut the slice into four squares.

Crack the egg into a basin. Add the milk and a good shake of salt
and pepper. Whisk them together with a fork.

Pour the egg and milk on to a dinner plate and lay the bread squares
in it. Turn them over several times until they have soaked up most
of the egg.

Put the knob of butter (large conker-sized) in a frying pan and put
it on the heat. The butter will melt, then start to go frothy. When
it does, lift the squares of bread with a fish slice, one at a time, and
lay them gently in the butter.

Keep the heat steady and fry the bread for about one minute. Lift the corner of one square with the fish slice and if it is golden brown, turn them all over to brown the other sides. Ask a grown-up to watch while you do this part.

When all sides are brown take the pan off the heat and lift the fried bread on to a small plate.

My Fried Bread should be eaten hot. It is very good with bacon or spaghetti rings.

Stand on something firm to reach the cooker.

Where did Momotara go
With a hoity-toity-tighty?
He went to lay the giants low,
The wicked ones and mighty.

What did Momotara take?
His monkey, dog and pheasant,
Some dumplings and an almond cake,
To make the journey pleasant.

PINK SUGAR ALMOND CAKE

2 large eggs
4 oz. caster sugar
4 oz. self-raising flour
4 oz. soft margarine (the kind packed in tubs)
$\frac{1}{2}$ teaspoon almond essence
Pink food colouring
For the top
1 heaped tablespoon flaked almonds
1 flat tablespoon caster sugar

Makes 1 big cake

Ask a grown-up to put the oven on at 350°F OR Mark 4 and show you how to line the bottom and sides of a 6″ round cake tin with greased greaseproof paper.

Crack the eggs carefully into a mixing bowl. Weigh the sugar, flour and margarine and put them in with the eggs. Then add the almond essence.

Stand the bowl on a low surface or sit with it on your lap, whichever you find easier. Now mix everything together with a wooden spoon, holding the spoon low down near the wide part.

When the mixture looks smooth and creamy (it will take about 5 minutes with rests) it is ready for the colouring.

Dip the skewer into the colouring and shake 6–10 drops into the mixture. Stir it until all the mix turns a rich pink. Now let a grown-up give it one brisk stir.

Spoon all the mixture into the tin, scraping it off the wooden spoon with a tablespoon. Make your hand quite wet and pat the mixture flat. Sprinkle the top with almonds then sugar.

Put the cake in the centre of the oven. It will rise and bake pale gold in about 50 minutes.

Use a thick cloth to take it out. Ask a grown-up to tip the cake on to a wire rack and carefully peel off the paper. Leave the cake for an hour to get cold.

Keep margarine in the warm kitchen before mixing.

Wash the dishes, wipe the dishes
Ring the bell for tea,
And three good wishes, three good kisses
I will give to thee.

INDEX TO RECIPES